P.O.W.E.R. TOOL FOR LIFE GOALS

P.O.W.E.R. TOOL

FOR *Life* GOALS

Amanda Craven

LENDAL PRESS

First published in 2022 by Lendal Press
Woodend, The Crescent, Scarborough, YO11 2PW
an imprint of Valley Press · lendalpress.com

ISBN 978-1-912436-77-4
Catalogue no. LP0011

Cover and graphics designed by Fitzpatrick Design
Text layout by Peter Barnfather
Edited by Lucy Carroll

Printed and bound in Great Britain
by TJ Books Limited

CONTENTS

I dedicate this book to my inspirational parents, Joe and Anne,
and to my amazing daughters, Lucy, Alice and Rose,
who patiently understood my need to regularly
disappear into my office to work and write.

With thanks to Giulio for letting me share
his story and to all my clients over the years for
allowing me to be part of their journey.

INTRO

'Can you help me grow a beard?'

A few years ago, when I was a newly trained hypnotherapist, I received a Facebook message from a man asking if I could help him to grow a beard. I actually thought it was a joke as I'd had a few 'wind-up' enquiries in the first few months of qualifying, but I decided that I would reply in my usual professional way, and we arranged a short phone consultation to establish whether we were 'a good fit'.

During that conversation, I understood how desperate this very genuine-sounding gentleman was to grow a beard. Giulio had tried, unsuccessfully, to grow one since his late teens, but at each attempt his unconscious habit of plucking out the hairs around his mouth created a very strange-shaped mass of stubbly hair. Once he realised what he'd done, and his girlfriend (later his wife) caught sight of the 'beard', he was dispatched to the bathroom to shave the whole thing off. And so it had gone on for decades. Hence the distressed Facebook message.

It took us just two hypnotherapy sessions to uncover and eliminate the root cause of this unfortunate habit, and over the next few weeks I was delighted to receive weekly photo updates of a very handsome beard. This 'goal' of having a beard was so much more than just growing facial hair; once he had achieved it, this lovely man stood taller, oozed confidence, lost weight, bought new clothes and thoroughly enjoyed his smart new look.

The chances are your goal or goals don't involve growing a beard, though they may be connected in some way to how you look – or how you feel about yourself. You might want to achieve 'something' – a qualification, a promotion, a new fitness level – or acquire 'a thing', like a house or car, for example. You might not even know what you want, but just 'know' that there's more out there and that you want some of it. Whatever 'it' may be.

And this is where I, and this book, come in.

I believe that **everyone** has the right – and the power – to change their life and to reach for the stars, if that's what they want. I have been honoured to help hundreds of clients who have wanted to create change in their life. Once clients work through any 'obstacles' (from anxiety to addictions, phobias to past trauma) they are ready to start a new chapter, follow their dreams, and become who they truly wanted to be. I want to accompany **you** on **your** life journey, too, and hear about the successes you're about to enjoy! Just like Giulio, and countless other fabulous human beings I have met. Like one amazing lady who came to see me with a fear of heights that had mushroomed over decades into agoraphobia and a complete lack of self-esteem. Her world had become a very small, yet scary, place. After our work together she celebrated her new lease of life by dyeing her hair purple (to the horror of her grandchildren) and her husband began commenting on the amount of petrol she now consumed as she confidently zipped around the countryside in the car that had spent much of its life till then on the driveway!

The techniques covered in this book have been developed through years of helping clients like the ones I've described above and have been the reason for my own goal-setting successes. Even before formalising the 5-step process I realised I had reached many of my life goals – getting my dream job abroad, achieving several promotions, starting my own business, moving to the seaside, and getting distinctions in my studies as a mature student, to name but a few – by intuitively taking the actions now defined in the P.O.W.E.R. TOOL FOR GOALS® process. It's also how I actually wrote this book and got a publishing deal! I have personally had to work through many challenges (including the untimely loss of my mum to cancer, getting cancer myself at forty-one, divorce, single-parenthood and financial difficulties) and self-sabotage issues (stemming from what I see now as a suffocating Catholic education in the 1970s). Having a structured framework was invaluable at these times and helped me to keep looking forwards.

This book gave me the opportunity to draw on all these personal and professional experiences and bring everything together 'under one roof' as an effective, easy to remember 5-step process that will also help YOU to change your life.

This P.O.W.E.R. TOOL FOR GOALS® method will therefore ensure that, whatever your goals or your desired changes, you have all the ingredients you need for your success.

How to use this book

Chapter 1 will guide you through a series of exercises to help you define your life goals. Once you have a clear idea of the changes you want to make, **Chapters 2 to 6** will walk you through the P.O.W.E.R. TOOL. To make this tool easy to remember, each of the five letters in the word 'POWER' represents a step of the process:

Picture Your Goal

Strategies for visualising your goals and dreams, plus the science behind this.

One Step at a Time

How to break each goal down into manageable steps and keep focused.

When Are You Doing This?

Understanding the importance of committing to time frames and ways to do this.

Evaluate and Measure Your Progress

Techniques to check in on the strategies you're using and assess whether you're on target.

Reason You Are Doing This

Understanding the importance of 'owning' your goals to keep your plans on track.

In order to optimise your success, I recommend that you cover the chapters in the following order: **1, 6, 2, 3, 4, 5**.

After working through these chapters, you will then be ready to create your very own **28-Day P.O.W.E.R. Action Plan (Chapter 7)**: a step-by-step guide that you can use to create a personalised week-by-week / month-by-month action plan, helping you to create goals you can smash. The tables in this chapter will cover the crucial first twenty-eight days, but your tools will enable you to take as long as you need. This plan covers up to three goals, but the tool is completely flexible, and you have everything you need to do more – or fewer – goals. You can download – for free – all of the tables from this book as many times as you like from:

resources.amandacraven.org/powertoolforlifegoals

If you get stuck at any point during the above stages, **Chapter 8 (Feeling Stuck?)** looks at the obstacles you may face when working towards goals and contains techniques and tips on how to overcome them.

Whenever you see the headphones icon (🎧) this means you can download an audio version of the text from the above website.

It's now time to get yourself a nice notebook (or folder for your printouts) and some coloured pens that you enjoy writing with, and make sure they're accessible at all times.

I hope you're as excited about your new chapter as I am for you! What are you waiting for?? Turn the page and let's get you started!!

WHAT DO YOU WANT TO CHANGE?

1

What's this chapter about?

This section is a chance to go under the bonnet by looking at why it's important for us to set goals and what we get from this process.

After that, there are five easy-to-do yet very powerful exercises that will help you create a working list of life goals for yourself.

We are wired to set goals

The fact of the matter is that we humans are wired to set goals for ourselves: to explore, stretch our capabilities, and generally to improve our lot. If we weren't, we'd still be living in caves with only our hands as tools.

In addition to the survival responses hard-wired into the oldest parts of our brain, humans have a large, well-developed and relatively 'modern' section called the pre-frontal cortex (PFC). It is our PFC which enables us to carry out many complex thought processes which include (amongst many other functions) evaluating the past, considering the present and actively planning the future. This is what distinguishes us from other animals. Researchers [1,2] have established that animals have a much smaller PFC and tend to *react* and adapt to their *immediate* environment and circumstances, lacking our pro-active, planning and appraisal abilities.

According to psychologist and goal-setting expert Edwin Locke, goals are a biological need for humans, fundamental to our survival *and* happiness.[3] This means that if we're not working

[1] Brian Kolb, *Do All Mammals Have a prefrontal Cortex?*, 2010

[2] Chad J. Donahue, *Quantitative Assessment of prefrontal Cortex in Humans relative to Nonhuman Primates*, 2018

[3] Edwin Locke & Gary Latham, *Enhancing the Benefits and Overcoming the Pitfalls of Goal Setting*, 2006

towards a future goal, we are under-performing. If we are just coasting through life or living each day like it's Groundhog Day, we will likely feel dissatisfied or uneasy, or have a vague feeling that something is lacking. But it's only when we stop and consciously take stock that we are able to identify what is lacking and be clear on what we want. And that's exactly what this first chapter will help you to do.

Before we move on to the different ways you can use this opportunity to identify and define your goals in the most effective way, let's just take a peek at all the benefits you will get from this process.

What do we get from goals?

Research has identified key benefits linked to goal setting, and it's interesting to note that we benefit most from setting **clear** goals that are **meaningful to us** and will **stretch us**.

So, what happens when we set, and achieve, our goals?

We...

- increase our self-esteem
- gain self-confidence
- tend to make more effort in all areas of our life
- improve our overall performance in life tasks
- boost our energy levels
- grow as a person
- fulfil our potential
- experience positive emotions and increase our general sense of wellbeing
- reduce boredom

- create a sense of purpose
- improve our ability to focus
- feel more satisfied and accomplished
- develop resilience and persistence

Studies have shown that setting goals leads to improvements in performance of all kinds – personal achievements, sporting events, exams, lifestyle. The action of goal setting creates a sense of purpose and a momentum that creates energy and powerful vibrations, which leads to more action, excitement and achievement.

It's like creating a blueprint for our brain or tapping the destination into our satnav. Once we clarify where we want to be, our brain will identify the best route to get us there and be on the lookout for alternatives should there be a holdup or a dead end. A satnav will only function if we are clear on where we want to go; just saying 'I want to go North' is of no use at all. Similarly, vaguely stating that you want to 'improve your lifestyle' is unlikely to move you forward.

Where do we start?

Do you remember the hype and excitement surrounding the early Apple launches engineered by Steve Jobs, which looked more like rock concerts than anything else? Or, more recently, the fever pitch surrounding Elon Musk's Tesla cars? This excitement wasn't because people already owned those products and were delighted with them – they only existed as prototypes during those early pre-launch rallies. Rather, the creators had a clear vision and plan which they communicated and shared with the public. It was, to all intents and purposes, just the ideas of these 'visionaries' that had been articulated in a way that influenced consumer opinion and made them want what they were selling, whatever the cost. Where the Tesla cars were concerned, Musk's vision and conviction meant that people were prepared to lay down $100,000 and wait (for over two years in some cases) in anticipation of owning one.[4]

This section is about generating YOUR ideas and the exercises will help you to get the clarity you need. You possibly don't want to create a billion-dollar business, but I bet you can think back to a time when you had an idea that made you feel excited and alive, even before it became a reality. Maybe you remember feeling that rush of energy and excitement after booking a holiday, deciding to move house, change your car or simply after deciding to change something about your appearance? That feeling of potential and anticipation can give us wings and can begin to create shifts in **all** areas of our life.

You may already have your goals in mind and have picked up this book to make it easier to make them happen. I suggest you work through the next part anyway, just as a way of checking in with yourself and your goals. There's no limit to the number of goals you can add to your list (we'll discuss how many you should work on at once later on) and you might find inspiration to work on areas you hadn't thought of.

If you haven't yet got specific goals in mind and are looking for inspiration, the following sections will give you plenty of ideas. So, set aside some quiet time to go through the suggestions and see what resonates with you. You don't have to complete every section, just the ones that 'speak' to you.

[4] Ashlee Vance, *Elon Musk: How the Billionaire CEO of SpaceX and Tesla is shaping our Future*, 2016

Whether you're a seasoned goal setter or a newbie, you can fill in the tables in this book (yes, you **can** write in this book – it is yours, and yours only!) or go to **resources.amandacraven.org/ powertoolforlifegoals** and download free printable copies of the tables. If you've managed to bag yourself a whole evening or afternoon to work on your goals, you can work through the rest of this chapter in one sitting. If, however, you're pushed for time, you can do the activities in ten-minute chunks. However, without putting yourself under too much pressure, try not to leave more than a couple of days between each 'chunk' or you will lose focus and momentum. Whichever way you're doing this, find somewhere comfy to sit, get yourself a cuppa and play some music you love. Enjoy the start of your journey!

Exercise 1.
Think about the changes
you want in all areas of your Life

Think about the following areas in your life and make notes in the table or in your notepad about any changes you'd like to make. I've added a few ideas to get you started:

Career or business:

- Do something different
- Get a second job
- Retrain in a new skill
- Change to a more / less challenging position
- Reduce / increase my hours
- Earn more money
- Start my own business
- Grow / downsize my existing business
- Diversify my business

Family life:

- Start a family
- Consider fostering or adoption
- Spend more time with my children
- Do more with my partner
- Spend more / less time with other family members
- Plan care for elderly relatives
- Get a pet

My home:

- Redecorate a room
- Re-arrange furniture
- Declutter a room
- Redesign my kitchen
- Buy / make soft furnishings
- Redesign my outdoor space

Personal relationships:

- Join a social club
- Start dating
- Have a break from dating
- Plan to move in together
- End a romance that's gone stale
- Invest more in friendships
- Eliminate any toxic friendships / relationships

Wellbeing and fitness:

- More me-time
- Book regular massages
- Find a sport / exercise I enjoy
- Eat better, start juicing
- Lose weight
- Learn a new sport
- Spend more time outdoors
- Reduce my anxiety

My appearance:

- New style of clothes
- Different hairstyle / colour
- Do my make-up differently
- Create a new overall image for myself

Hobbies and pastimes:

- Spend more time doing a hobby
- Starting a collection of something that interests me
- Join an evening class
- Set aside time each week to learn a new skill
- Join a choir
- Learn an instrument
- Write fiction or poetry
- Make videos about my hobby to share online

Big purchases:

- House or flat
- Holiday home
- Office
- Garden shed
- Computer or tablet
- New kitchen
- Car or motorbike
- Photography equipment
- Recording studio

Finances:

- Increase my income
- Start saving
- Plan my pension
- Re-invest my savings
- Make a will
- Plan for my kids' studies
- Make charity donations

Studies:

- Start a part-time or full-time study program (online / in-person / blended)
- Defer an application
- Take a sabbatical

Travels:

- Plan a mini break
- Book a holiday at home or abroad
- Research themed vacations (e.g., art / cookery / yoga)
- Take a year out
- Plan a three-month tour

Spirituality:

- Take up mediation
- Join a religious or spiritual group
- Read books that inspire me
- Start journaling

Community / volunteer work:

- Become more active in my neighbourhood
- Babysit or granny-sit
- Befriend someone who is housebound
- Offer to walk my neighbours' dogs
- Volunteer in a charity shop / local charity
- Arrange regular donations (time or money) to specific charities

EXERCISE 1 NOTES

Use this table to make notes of changes you want:

CAREER OR BUSINESS	
FAMILY LIFE	
YOUR HOME OR GARDEN	
PERSONAL RELATIONSHIPS	
WELLBEING & FITNESS	
YOUR APPEARANCE	
HOBBIES & PASTIMES	
BIG PURCHASES	
FINANCES	
STUDIES	
TRAVELS	
SPIRITUALITY	
COMMUNITY/ VOLUNTEER WORK	

Exercise 2.
Find a role model

Studies have shown that recalling a person who would support us in our pursuit of a goal can positively contribute to our success.[5] This could even be your 'future self' – we will explore this idea more in the next chapter.

Are there any role models you have and could use as inspiration? They may be people you actually know or know of, or people who are successful in sports, entertainment, business, or other walks of life. I have many role models that inspire me in my work and my life, from successful trail-blazing life coaches to public figures who have brought joy to the masses. My two perennial favourites are country singer and entrepreneur Dolly Parton and Scottish comedian and actor Billy Connolly. Both have overcome less than ideal starts in life to live the way they dreamed of, teaching themselves to be comfortable and confident in their own skin. Who inspires you? Use the following space to make a few notes.

[5]   Edwin Locke & Gary Latham, *New Developments in Goal Setting and Task Performance* (Chapter 9), 2013

Role model name:

What you admire about them or what they have that you would like:

Role model name:

What you admire about them or what they have that you would like:

Role model name:

What you admire about them or what they have that you would like:

Exercise 3.
Think about what you DON'T want

You might find the following approach useful if you're struggling to define your goals.

Begin by making a list of things you're unhappy with, for example:

- I never have enough money to buy what I want
- I'm fed up with my job
- I hate not having a garden
- I don't get enough time for myself
- I hate the way I look
- I'm sick of worrying about paying the bills every month
- I don't like being on my own
- I'm bored in the evenings

Now make a positive goal statement by saying the opposite (positively framing your goals leads to better outcomes), for example:

- I want to earn more money
- I want to change my job
- I want some outdoor space
- I want more me-time
- I want to improve my appearance
- I want to reduce my bills
- I want to find a partner
- I want to develop some new hobbies

You're ready to define your goal, for example:

- I'm going to earn an extra £/$10,000 this year
- I'm going to apply for another job
- I'm going to get a house with a garden or rent a plot of land
- I'm going to set aside more time for myself each week
- I'm going to lose weight and experiment with different styles of clothes
- I'm going to research the best deals and change my service suppliers
- I'm going to start dating
- I'm going to try out some new pastimes

You can use the blank table to help develop your goals, like in this example:

EXAMPLE TABLE

	WHAT YOU'RE UNHAPPY WITH/ WANT TO CHANGE	POSITIVE GOAL STATEMENT	DEFINED GOAL
A	I never have enough money to buy what I want	I want to earn more money	I'm going to earn an extra £/$10 000 this year
B	I'm fed up with my job	I want to change my job	I'm going to apply for another job
C	I hate not having a garden	I want some outdoor space	I'm going to get a house with a garden or rent a plot of land
D	I don't get enough time for myself	I want more me-time	I'm going to set aside more me-time each week
E	I hate the way I look	I want to improve my appearance	I'm going to lose weight and experiment with different styles of clothes
F	My monthly bills are too high	I want to reduce my bills	I'm going to research the best deals and change my service suppliers
G	I'm fed up being on my own	I want to find a partner	I'm going to start dating
H	I'm bored in the evenings	I want to find some new hobbies	I'm going to try out some new pastimes

FOR YOU TO USE

	WHAT YOU'RE UNHAPPY WITH/ WANT TO CHANGE	POSITIVE GOAL STATEMENT	DEFINED GOAL
A			
B			
C			
D			
E			
F			
G			
H			

Exercise 4.
Write your bucket list

According to Tracie White writing in Stanford Medicine, a bucket list is 'a list of things you'd like to do before you die, like visiting Paris or running a marathon. It's a chance to think about the future and put lifelong dreams or long-term goals down on a piece of paper.'[6] White was reporting on a study that explored the health value of bucket lists; when doctors were made aware of a patient's goals, they were able to use them to motivate people with diseases and conditions that could be improved by lifestyle changes. For example, encouraging someone with diabetes to keep their sugar intake low now so that they could enjoy some of their son's wedding cake in a few months' time rather than simply saying 'You have to stop eating sugar' was found to be far more effective.

Bucket lists can cover anything from travel dreams, personal challenges (like a marathon or a skydive), or financial goals, to reaching milestone birthdays and celebrations.

Writing your bucket list here is a great way to focus your mind on future goals.

[6] Tracey White, *Talking to Doctors about your Bucket List Could Advance Care Planning*, 2018

My bucket list

Exercise 5.
Create a vision board

According to a study in 2016, creating a vision board can help us to reach our goals more easily. Oprah Winfrey used them for a long time, until she just naturally created visions of what she wanted in her head and did what was needed to make – or let – it happen.[7] She now describes herself as a very powerful 'manifester' (someone who makes their dreams become reality) and I believe her success speaks for itself!

We'll talk a lot more about the power of visualising your goals in the next chapter but creating a vision board can be a fantastic way of getting the ball rolling. Remember that nothing is set in stone and that any lists or boards you create are there to help you check in with how it all feels to you. Once you start to collect pictures, you may find that some ideas of things you initially wanted will change. And that's absolutely fine. This is a *process* – you aren't producing a masterpiece for anyone – and it will always be a work in progress!

So, what exactly is a vision board? Well, it can be a real 'board' (like a notice board) that you fill with photos, pictures, colours, cut-outs of words or sayings that are meaningful or inspiring to you. If you don't have a board, you could use part of a cardboard box or stick a few sheets of A4 paper together

[7]   Lisa Burton and Jonathan Lent, *The Use of Vision Boards as a Therapeutic Intervention*, 2016

to create a bigger surface. Some people do their vision boards on a tablet or computer – there are apps you can use (just search 'vision board' in your app store) or try Pinterest. I use plain A3 artist pad sheets or sometimes just open a blank document page and cut and paste pictures I've found. You can, of course, have as many boards as you like – it can be a good idea to have a few on the go in the early stages and create more focused boards as you go along.

If you're able to display your board(s) somewhere you can see them every day, they are definitely more effective and enable you to understand how connected you are to these ideas. For example, if a picture of a sleek modern kitchen or an allotment bursting with colourful fruit and vegetables makes you grin from ear to ear each time you see it, you'll know you're on the right track.

If you like the idea of a vision board but don't know where to start, you might want to check out ideas on YouTube (again, just type 'vision board' into the search box) or use the following as prompts:

- Magazine or newspaper pictures of role models, aspirational homes or lifestyles
- Holiday brochure photos
- Your favourite words or quotes (you can write these out or print them in arty fonts)
- Your old photos – let your younger self inspire you
- Colours from paint charts that generate a strong reaction or emotion
- Instagram or other social media posts of people or organisations that you feel connected to
- Song lyrics that resonate with you
- Your environment – go out and about to take pictures of scenes and places that make you feel good

Wrapping things up

Congratulations! You're ready to create your working list. Look through all your ideas above and extract up to ten goals that you can add to the list at the end of this chapter or on your printout. You may have ended up with more than ten so you can keep a note of the others to revisit at a later date.

The following chapters can pretty much be worked through in order, with the exception of **Chapter 6** (Reason for your goals) which I recommend you read now.

Once you've read **Chapter 6**, you'll be ready to dive into the visualisation techniques in **Chapter 2** and move forward from there. Strategies from both these chapters will help you throughout your P.O.W.E.R. TOOL process.

MY GOALS LIST

PICTURE IT!

2

What's this chapter about?

This In this chapter, we'll take a peek at the scientific *and* anecdotal evidence about using 'imagery'* in goal setting.

You'll then have some fun exercises to help you 'picture' your own goals. These exercises, together with your work on why you want these things in your life (from **Chapter 6**) will make it easier for you to create a shortlist of around 3 goals and work towards your action plan.

---

*   Please note that although I use the word 'image' a lot this is a very generic term and refers to any sort of impression we can have in our mind. Some people are naturally very 'visual', seeing very clear pictures of people and events in their mind's eye like they're looking at a photo or watching a film. Others get more of a vague 'impression' of what they're thinking about and may be aware of feelings, sounds – even smells – more than actual images, and sometimes might even just 'see' black, or nothing at all.

You don't have to be 'visual' to do these exercises! However, your goals show up in your imagination is just fine!

The power of visualisation

A picture paints more than a thousand words! Images can communicate ideas, feelings or concepts that sometimes can't even be put into words. We create pictures in our mind from our subconscious – a place where there are no limits and where critical thought has no place. This ability is another key part of being human and differentiates us once more from other members of the animal kingdom.

The power of visualisation has been recognised for millennia and has been harnessed for healing and self-improvement purposes since the time of sleep temples in the ancient world, right through to hypnotherapy in the present day.

In *The Evolution of Imagination*, Stephen Asma wrote that 'human culture itself is impossible without the imagination' and, indeed, since time immemorial, writers, philosophers and leaders have described events, dreams and shared knowledge that have enabled us to create pictures in our own mind.[8] From these images we have been able to learn, grow or escape into imaginary worlds. J.K. Rowling created Harry Potter and his magical world in her mind before she was able to put it into words. Artists, composers, inventors and engineers visualise the outcome of their works long before there is anything to see in the 'real' world. Successful film directors 'see' scenes in their

---

[8] Stephen Asma, *The Evolution of Imagination*, 2017

mind's eye before being able to communicate directions to actors and bring the story to life. We have already touched on the powerful visions of Oprah Winfrey, Steve Jobs and Elon Musk in **Chapter 1**, and to write a list of other successful 'visionaries' past and present would take all the pages of this book!

Scientists refer to 'visualisation' or 'creating pictures in our imagination' as 'mental imagery', and many experimental studies have shown the positive impact of such techniques on goal setting, including increasing motivation and pleasure in achieving goals, as well as increasing positive outcomes.[9, 10, 11]

Studies of the brain have even proved that our image-thoughts can directly impact our body. Amazingly, whilst sitting or lying down and without physically moving, the 'mental rehearsal' of techniques – ranging from playing chess or the piano, to developing muscles and perfecting golf swings – actually translates into real-life improvements, physical changes and record achievements. The reason? Our brain doesn't differentiate between what we see in our mind's eye and physical reality!

Visualisation before a competition or a match is now regularly undertaken by elite athletes who often hire psychologists or coaches specialising in this practice – Tiger Woods, Jack

[9] For example: Krista Munroe-Chandler and Michelle Guerrero, *Psychological Imagery in Sport and Performance*, 2017

[10] Fritz Renner et al, *Mental Imagery as a 'motivational amplifier' to Promote Activities*, 2019

[11] Fritz Renner et al, *Effects of Engaging in Repeated Mental Imagery of Future Positive Events on Behavioural Activation in Individuals with Major Depressive Disorder*, 2017

Nicklaus, Arnold Schwarzenegger, Michael Phelps and Katie Ledecky are all open about having used it. Away from the sports arena, Oprah Winfrey has used visualisation to achieve her goals throughout her career and now focuses more and more on the power of our mind-body in her shows. When Jim Carrey, now a successful actor and multi-millionaire, was struggling to scrape a living, he used to drive round the wealthy areas of town and picture himself living there. He famously wrote himself a cheque for $10 million ('for acting services rendered') and dated it 5 years from then as a way of defining his goal. Within a few days of that five-year deadline (Thanksgiving 1995, in case you're curious!), he received a $10 million contract for the film *Dumb and Dumber*. Just imagine that!

So, hopefully YOU are now convinced about the importance and value of picturing your goals and will enjoy the following exercises designed to guide you through simple – yet powerful – ways of using **your** imagination and **your** ability to picture your goals.

I know it's tempting to skip through exercises in books like this and 'just get on with it', but each one only takes a few minutes and will really impact on the successful outcome of your goals.

Test your imagination

As mentioned above, the human mind has the most incredible ability to create 'images' which we don't only see in our mind's eye but can feel and experience with all of our senses. To help you understand the power and depth of this ability to visualise, we're going to do two short exercises.

Exercise 1. (🎧)
Notice the impact of 'negative' imagery

Think back to the last time you worried about something or felt very angry with someone.

Or maybe a time when a loved one hadn't arrived home at the expected time, you had a near miss in the car, or you regretted something you said at a meeting or night out.

Maybe someone hurt or betrayed you in some way, lied to you, or deliberately excluded you from an event.

Close your eyes for a minute and remember this event with as much detail as possible.

- Where were you?
- What were you wearing?
- What could you see, hear or smell?
- What were you thinking?
- Who else was there?
- What was being said – or implied?
- How did you feel, emotionally and physically?

Just stay with these feelings for a few moments before opening your eyes.

When you re-open your eyes, just notice how you feel. Are your fists or teeth clenched? Do you feel angry or sad? Do you recall all the 'what if' scenarios you went through, the ruminations, recriminations, and the way your heart rate speeded up, your breathing changed, or how you felt sick or light-headed?

. . .

Take a few deep breaths before doing the next exercise.

Exercise 2. (🎧)
Notice the impact of 'positive' imagery

Now, think back to an event or a time when you felt good in some way. Maybe you achieved something you worked hard for, like getting a new job, or learning a new skill. Perhaps you have happy memories of a holiday, your wedding or partnership ceremony. It could just be a moment of relaxation – a lie in or a lazy day.

Just go to the first example that comes to mind and close your eyes again. Remember where you were, who was there, and how everyone was dressed.

- What was the weather like?
- What sounds could you hear?
- Were you moving or still?
- Were you laughing, talking loudly or quiet?

Stay with that scene for a few minutes. When you re-open your eyes, pay attention to how your body is feeling now.

- How does it compare to just a few minutes ago?

As far as your brain was concerned the events happening in your imagination in both these exercises were just as real as if they actually happened. And your body reacted just as it would in real time. This is how powerful mental imagery is!

A blueprint for your future

Another example of the power of visualisation is a phenomenon known as the 'frequency illusion'. Can you think of a time when you were considering a new purchase, say a new car or phone? You decide on a certain make / model / colour, and then you suddenly notice these cars / phones all around you. Or maybe you were unhappy in your relationship, or single and looking for love. The world is suddenly full of loving couples who appear to be living the dream. Everywhere you look. And you wonder how you didn't see them before! In actual fact, whilst you were doing your research or dreaming about your 'perfect' match, you created a narrow focus on that specific product or on your desire for love. The result was that your brain had established a sort of blueprint and was on the lookout for things that matched and fitted in with those images.

This is how the process works when you visualise your goals. The more 'mind pictures' you make, the easier it becomes for your brain to look out for opportunities to make those goals happen!

A new car

Just before I wrote this book, I decided I was going to get a brand-new car (for the first time in my life – I'd only ever bought used cars until then) by a certain date. I pictured myself driving around in a new car, bigger than my current car, and enjoying all the perks you get with the latest model. I got COVID-19 in the interim and didn't have the energy to do much at all about any of my goals.

About two weeks before the 'deadline' I'd set myself, I was well enough to sit up and do bits and bobs on my laptop. I noticed some incredible interest-free offers for buying the next model up of my current car that were popping up on my computer. I decided to mull it over and then a couple of days later, once I got my voice back, I called the garage. We went through a questionnaire to see if I was eligible for the deal, but I wasn't very hopeful as my earnings weren't particularly high at that point, and I was amazed to then hear the salesman say, 'Great. That's gone through! What colour would you like?'

The monthly payments were the same amount as the ones I'd been paying for my current (now five-year-old) car that was starting to need work doing on it, and they offered more than I expected for aforementioned car as part exchange. Whilst I was scrolling the colour options, the salesman phoned me back and said he'd just had an email from the head office offering an extra incentive to existing customers of the garage (that was me) of £1000 cashback. It was just getting better and better. I decided that I was going to use the cashback to get iPads for my daughters who had been desperate for them for years, but I'd never been able to indulge them.

In short, within five days of my deadline I was driving around in the most amazing new car I'd ever had, and it felt so right – just as it had in my visualisations. Not on the same scale as Jim Carrey's success (yet!) but an amazing win for me nevertheless! Despite feeling woolly-headed from being ill, my brain had been on the lookout for ways to make my goal a reality and presented me with the opportunities I needed. No-one had been going to pull up outside my house in a brand-new car and hand me the keys just because I wished for one, but the combination of stating a clearly defined goal, visualising it, AND taking action meant that it happened.

Hundreds of clients have used my guided mental imagery techniques to achieve promotions, pass exams, travel, carry out public speaking engagements and set up businesses amongst many other life changes. Once their goals were visualised, the action steps they needed to take also became so much clearer. One lady had come to me because her daughter was getting married, and she didn't think she could cope with her ex-husband and his new wife also being there. We did lots of mental rehearsing as well as some clearing work, and she wrote to me after the big day saying she felt like she was in a film, and everything unfolded beautifully, just as it had in her imagination!

My own visions of using the P.O.W.E.R. TOOL to help lots more people to live the life they deserve than I could just coaching 1-1, and of sitting on ITV's Lorraine's sofa talking to her about this book, have kept me excited and motivated throughout the writing process. To paraphrase Jim Carrey again, you can't just think of a goal, picture it, then go and eat a sandwich. You need to act on it! And we'll just have to wait and see whether I get to check out Lorraine's sofa. (I wonder if Oprah would also like a chat…)

• • •

Aherm! Right, I'll stop daydreaming for a moment! Are YOU ready to get the ball rolling and visualise **your** goals? Yes? Great. **Exercises 3, 4 and 5** will help you do just that. Let's go!

Exercise 3. (🧠)
Visualise your goal

If you haven't already created a vision board, you might want to do one now – see **Exercise 5** in **Chapter 1** for ideas. Otherwise, you can just focus on one of your goals from your list at the end of Chapter 1.

Focus on images (or words) for **one** of your goals for a few moments, taking in all the details. Imagine you're actually there, having achieved your goal.

Notice...

- where you are
- anything you can see around you
- what you're wearing
- how you're feeling
- the expression on your face
- how you're standing or moving
- how your voice sounds
- who else is there
- what they are doing

Think about your breath and imagine breathing in the scene before your eyes, letting it expand inside you so it takes up all the space it can, and then breathing out any obstacles that come up, so your image gets bigger and stronger.

When you're ready, close your eyes. Keep exploring everything connected with your goal that comes up. Take as long as you need – I suggest at least five minutes – then gently re-open your eyes and ground yourself by pressing your feet into the floor or your hands into the chair or bed.

Now make notes of what came up for you, whether it felt positive or negative. Your gut reaction is a vital guide and we'll be checking in with it a lot as we work through the P.O.W.E.R. TOOL. Here are some questions to prompt you:

- How did you feel having achieved your goal?
- Was everything as you imagined it to be?
- What thoughts or emotions did you have?
- Did you feel energised or relaxed?
- What did you notice in your body?
- Could you see what else you might need for this goal to be achieved?
- Did any other goals come up – as well as or instead of this one?

Exercise 4.
Record your future success

Repeat **Exercise 3** for up to five goals, making notes for each one. If you want to print off extra copies of your goals notes go to:

resources.amandacraven.org/powertoolforlifegoals

Don't avoid or ignore feelings that come up for you as you think about your goals – any feedback is invaluable and will guide you through both setting and achieving your goals. It's vital to keep checking in with yourself so you can adjust your course as you go along. Uncomfortable or even painful feelings are your mind's way of letting you know that this may not be right for you, or that there's an obstacle and something needs to be cleared, worked through, or released so you can move forward. We'll cover this in depth in **Chapter 7** – 'Feeling Stuck?'.

NOTES

> **EXAMPLE GOAL:** *To travel to South America.*
>
> *It felt amazing to be walking through the Andes with a group of people. I was exhilarated and so confident. I was tanned, looked and felt fit and healthy and felt like I was literally exploding with happiness and a sense of making my dreams come true. I definitely want to do this!*

GOAL:

GOAL:

GOAL:

GOAL:

GOAL:

Exercise 5.
Writing a letter from your future self

Begin by focusing your attention on one of your goals at a time. Bring back an image of you having achieved this goal in as much detail as possible. Close your eyes for a few moments if it helps you to focus. Now imagine this 'future you' is having a conversation with you today.

- What would 'future you' be saying?
- What encouragement would you have?
- How would you describe your life now that those goals have been achieved?

Imagine this conversation in the present tense ('I am healthy and full of energy', 'I'm debt-free and am so much more relaxed').

You can either continue to visualise this exchange or open your eyes and write down these thoughts, as though 'future you' is writing you a letter. Don't forget to date it in the future!

Date

Place

Dear

It feels SO amazing now that I have achieved my goals!
My life feels so different and I am

I KNOW that you can do this, and hope you remember to enjoy the

journey as well as these fabulous end results!

I'm really proud of you already and will be with you every step.

Yours truly

PS

Wrapping things up

Now that you have anchored some powerful 'pictures' of how your desired life-changes will look, you can work through the other steps until you're ready to set up your action plan. First, go to **Chapter 6** to confirm your reasons to set these goals, then do **Chapters 3, 4 and 5** in order.

Remember that you can practise visualisations throughout the process to check that you're on the right track.

ONE STEP AT A TIME

3

What's this chapter about?

Focus is a crucial part of your success so we're going to look at why it matters, and how you can break each goal down into subgoals and tiny steps that are easy to target and achieve.

The exercises in this chapter provide a step-by-step guide to your individual goal-setting process, making it all feel easy and manageable.

What's wrong with multi-tasking?!

It's official! Multi-tasking is a myth. **Even** for women!! What we are actually doing when we think we're doing several things at the same time is simply switching focus from one thing to another. We can of course, for example, do DIY or crafting whilst listening to the radio – each activity is using a different 'internal resource' (i.e., listening and directing hand-eye coordination in this case) – but even then, if our attention is grabbed by a song we love or an interview with someone we admire, our ability to continue the manual task is, at best, significantly slowed down. Often progress is completely halted for the time we actively pay attention to the sounds. Then we go back to our manual task, usually unaware of the switch.

In addition to being limited to using one 'internal' resource at a time (listening, speaking, writing, drawing, using our arms / feet etc.) we **all** have limited 'external' resources available to us. The main external resources that we need to achieve our goals include time, energy, skills, information, money, equipment, support, and physical space. All these resources need to be allocated in the most efficient way and this is where good planning (i.e., using this P.O.W.E.R. TOOL FOR GOALS®) comes in!

Before we begin the task of breaking down our goals into small, manageable chunks, we need to look at our goals from an objective perspective. Why? Because this will help us see any patterns in our goals that will help us plan better and maximise **all** our resources. It will also help us create the focus we need.

Researchers have identified 3 types of goals:

EXAMPLE: TYPES OF GOALS

Researchers have identified 3 types of goals

1. SEPARATE: UNCONNECTED GOALS

GOAL 1: LEARNING A NEW MUSICAL INSTRUMENT

GOAL 2: WRITING A FICTION BOOK

GOAL 3: STUDYING FOR A PROFESSIONAL QUALIFICATION

| GOAL 1 | GOAL 2 | GOAL 3 |

2. SEQUENTIAL: GOALS THAT NATURALLY FOLLOW ON FROM OTHERS

GOAL 1: PASSING AN EXAM

SO YOU CAN... GOAL 2: GET A BETTER PAID JOB

AND THEN... GOAL 3: BUY A HOUSE

GOAL 1 → GOAL 2 → GOAL 3

3. RECIPROCAL: GOALS THAT MUTUALLY BENEFIT EACH OTHER

GOAL 1: LOSING WEIGHT

GOAL 2: IMPROVING PHYSICAL FITNESS

GOAL 3: IMPROVING MENTAL HEALTH

GOAL 1 — GOAL 2 — GOAL 3

Remember that one goal type is not better than another – the preparation process will be slightly different for each one, and the planning and execution of **Type 1** goals can take a bit more time as there is less synergy. If you have lots of goals and can pick and choose the order in which you do them, you might find it easier to start with **Type 2** or **Type 3**.

> **TIP.** Being clear about the *type* of goals you're aiming for will help you make best use of all your resources and make it easier to plan and prioritise your actions.

Being specific about the goal or the step creates focus (similar to the 'frequency illusion' I mentioned in **Chapter 2**) and makes it easier for us to prioritise what we do. The more clarity we have the easier it is for our brain to look out for helpful information, resources and opportunities. As I already mentioned above, this process will continue even for the goals we have put on the 'back burner' for now, with our subconscious mind scanning for things that fit in with all our life goals. The focus we work on in this chapter means we are also more likely to take action and make the effort required.[12] Being specific in defining each step also makes it easier to gain relevant measures & feedback so we can see how well we're doing (more of that in **Chapter 5. Evaluate and Measure Your Progress**).

[12] Edwin Locke & Gary Latham, *New Developments in Goal Setting and Task Performance* (Chapter 1), 2013

Exercise 1.
A closer look at your goals

Go back and look at your list of goals from the end of **Chapter 1**. Write them down in Box A below. Look at them with fresh eyes. Are they connected in any way? If you achieve one, will it help you move towards the other(s)? Some goals may be 'end goals', some may be 'subgoals' (steps that clearly lead to an 'end goal') so you can group them together if this is the case and count them as one goal. I like to use different colour pens to do this grouping.

Now underline up to three goals (or grouped goals) that seem to be the most urgent/important/appealing or the ones with the most synergy. If there are any left over you can revisit them later, once the action steps for these first three goals have become part of your regular routine, or once you have completed them.

Make a note of what goal type they are in your **Goal Type** table.

MY EXAMPLE GOALS

Earn more money

Write this book

Learn to play ukuele

Contribute more to Dad's care

Create a nice outdoor space

Renovate bathroom

Do more 'cultural' things
(visit stately homes etc)

Create new 'style' for self

Spend more time with children

Eat out more

MY EXAMPLE GROUPED GOALS

Earn more money

Write this book

Learn to play ukulele

Contribute more to Dad's care

Create a nice outdoor space

Renovate bathroom

Do more 'cultural' things (visit stately homes etc)

Create new 'style' for self

Spend more time with children

Eat out more

So, I decided that I would focus on:

- Increasing my income
- Spending more time with my children
- Writing this book

I knew that earning more money would enable me to make a financial contribution to my dad's care and afford renovations to my house. The other goals were on my radar now, so I would subconsciously be looking out for ways to make them happen, more as a 'side hustle' until I had time to properly focus on them.

Exercise 2.
Identify your sub-goals

Now you're ready to zoom in a bit more on your chosen goals and things you'll need to do to make them happen!

Make a note of which type your goals are and write this at the top of the **Goal Type** table. Put your three goals in the header boxes and for each one write down all the subgoals that you need to achieve. Your subgoals are all the different things you know you need to do to make your goal happen. It might help to close your eyes, focus on one goal at a time, and see what ideas come to you. Don't worry about the order of the sub-goals for now, and don't go into too much detail. Just get them written down. The next table gives you examples of my subgoals:

GOAL TYPE: **SEPARATE (TYPE 1)**

	GOAL 1 EARN MORE MONEY	GOAL 2 TIME WITH CHILDREN	GOAL 3 WRITE THIS BOOK
SUB GOALS	Get a business mentor	Tweak working hours to be more available when they get in from school	Research publishers
	Select social media platforms	Re-establish movie night	Explore self-publishing
	Clearly define all services	Have more meals together	Write overview of P.O.W.E.R. TOOL
	Create 'ideal' client profiles	Stop looking at phone or PC screen when they are talking to me	Get professionally designed logos
	Update website	Organise 1 day out each month	Register P.O.W.E.R. TOOL as trademark
	Work on SEO (Search Engine Optimization)	Eat out together once a month	Outline for each chapter
	Set up email marketing	Spend one-to-one time with each child	Draft each chapter
	Create digital marketing plan	Get some sporty/active games to play with console/TV together	Create videos and podcasts to accompany book
	Explore new services & products	Take them shopping more	Submit to publisher
			Set up companion website

GOAL TYPE:

	GOAL 1	GOAL 2	GOAL 3
SUB GOALS			

Exercise 3.
Your goal types and game plan

Now that you have a clearer idea of what you're going to need to do, it's time to decide on your game plan.

If your goals are **Type 1**: you need to decide whether it's possible to work at all three goals from the start, allocating different times to each one. If that doesn't feel feasible, look at any time constraints e.g., course or exam dates or gigs booked, so you can work out which goal you're going to focus on first. You could just choose the one you prefer, or the one that is going to be the easiest to start!

If they are **Type 2**: the sequence in which you tackle your goals should be obvious, so just make sure you focus on them in the right order.

If they are **Type 3**: you need to think about whether you will divide your time equally between your goals, or whether there is one that needs tackling first (or needs more time) in order to create momentum for the others.

Record your strategy in the box on the next page.

It's Your Call!

☐ I'm going to start all my goals at the same time

☐ I'm going to work on my goals in the following order:

1.

2.

3.

Exercise 4.
Creating your tiny steps

Now you're ready to break each goal into the tiniest steps so you can add them to your **Action Plan** in **Chapter 8**.

Take the subgoals from each goal above, add them to the blank **Goals/Tiny Steps** tables and divide each one into the smallest possible steps – aim for ten-minute chunks where possible. In some cases, you might need to do the same thing each day (like ten minutes daily guitar practice or switching your phone off). Just note it down once in this table and you'll put all the repeats into your action plan.

Don't worry if you don't fill every box; as long as you have broken everything down into the smallest actions, you have done enough! I've put some examples from my goals in the table on the next page.

(Remember, you can print off extra copies of all the tables in this book on: **resources.amandacraven.org/powertoolforlifegoals**)

EXAMPLE: TINY STEPS

GOAL: EARN MORE MONEY

SUB-GOAL: GET BUSINESS MENTOR

TINY STEPS

1	Ask for recommendations	☐	6	Look at return on investment	☐
2	Research on internet	☐	7	Draft business summary	☐
3	Check reviews	☐	8	Book meeting(s)	☐
4	Arrange preliminary chats	☐	9	Draft business goals	☐
5	Work out budget	☐	10	Prepare for meeting	☐

GOAL: MORE TIME WITH CHILDREN

SUB-GOAL: SPEND 1-1 TIME WITH EACH CHILD

TINY STEPS

1	Share my plans	☐	6	Set budget	☐
2	Ask each one to write list of things to do	☐	7	Arrange care for other children	☐
3	Ask on Facebook for ideas	☐	8	Make list of equipment (eg craft stuff)	☐
4	Agree best days/dates	☐	9	Order 'equipment'	☐
5	Put on calendar	☐	10	Switch phone off	☐

GOAL: PUBLISH THIS BOOK

SUB-GOAL: FIND PUBLISHER

TINY STEPS

1	Ask for recommendations	☐	6	Define target reader	☐
2	Research on internet	☐	7	Prepare for meeting	☐
3	Check current publications	☐	8	Find similar books & make list of publishers	☐
4	Check submission guidelines	☐	9		☐
5	Submit script	☐	10		☐

◎ GOAL 1

SUB-GOAL:

TINY STEPS

1 ☐   6 ☐
2 ☐   7 ☐
3 ☐   8 ☐
4 ☐   9 ☐
5 ☐   10 ☐

SUB-GOAL:

TINY STEPS

1 ☐   6 ☐
2 ☐   7 ☐
3 ☐   8 ☐
4 ☐   9 ☐
5 ☐   10 ☐

SUB-GOAL:

TINY STEPS

1 ☐   6 ☐
2 ☐   7 ☐
3 ☐   8 ☐
4 ☐   9 ☐
5 ☐   10 ☐

SUB-GOAL:

TINY STEPS

1 ☐   6 ☐
2 ☐   7 ☐
3 ☐   8 ☐
4 ☐   9 ☐
5 ☐   10 ☐

SUB-GOAL:

TINY STEPS

1 ☐   6 ☐
2 ☐   7 ☐
3 ☐   8 ☐
4 ☐   9 ☐
5 ☐   10 ☐

SUB-GOAL:

TINY STEPS

1 ☐ 6 ☐
2 ☐ 7 ☐
3 ☐ 8 ☐
4 ☐ 9 ☐
5 ☐ 10 ☐

SUB-GOAL:

TINY STEPS

1 ☐ 6 ☐
2 ☐ 7 ☐
3 ☐ 8 ☐
4 ☐ 9 ☐
5 ☐ 10 ☐

SUB-GOAL:

TINY STEPS

1 ☐ 6 ☐
2 ☐ 7 ☐
3 ☐ 8 ☐
4 ☐ 9 ☐
5 ☐ 10 ☐

SUB-GOAL:

TINY STEPS

1 ☐ 6 ☐
2 ☐ 7 ☐
3 ☐ 8 ☐
4 ☐ 9 ☐
5 ☐ 10 ☐

SUB-GOAL:

TINY STEPS

1 ☐ 6 ☐
2 ☐ 7 ☐
3 ☐ 8 ☐
4 ☐ 9 ☐
5 ☐ 10 ☐

◎ GOAL 2

SUB-GOAL:

TINY STEPS

1	☐	6	☐
2	☐	7	☐
3	☐	8	☐
4	☐	9	☐
5	☐	10	☐

SUB-GOAL:

TINY STEPS

1	☐	6	☐
2	☐	7	☐
3	☐	8	☐
4	☐	9	☐
5	☐	10	☐

SUB-GOAL:

TINY STEPS

1	☐	6	☐
2	☐	7	☐
3	☐	8	☐
4	☐	9	☐
5	☐	10	☐

SUB-GOAL:

TINY STEPS

1	☐	6	☐
2	☐	7	☐
3	☐	8	☐
4	☐	9	☐
5	☐	10	☐

SUB-GOAL:

TINY STEPS

1	☐	6	☐
2	☐	7	☐
3	☐	8	☐
4	☐	9	☐
5	☐	10	☐

SUB-GOAL:

TINY STEPS

1 ☐   6 ☐
2 ☐   7 ☐
3 ☐   8 ☐
4 ☐   9 ☐
5 ☐   10 ☐

SUB-GOAL:

TINY STEPS

1 ☐   6 ☐
2 ☐   7 ☐
3 ☐   8 ☐
4 ☐   9 ☐
5 ☐   10 ☐

SUB-GOAL:

TINY STEPS

1 ☐   6 ☐
2 ☐   7 ☐
3 ☐   8 ☐
4 ☐   9 ☐
5 ☐   10 ☐

SUB-GOAL:

TINY STEPS

1 ☐   6 ☐
2 ☐   7 ☐
3 ☐   8 ☐
4 ☐   9 ☐
5 ☐   10 ☐

SUB-GOAL:

TINY STEPS

1 ☐   6 ☐
2 ☐   7 ☐
3 ☐   8 ☐
4 ☐   9 ☐
5 ☐   10 ☐

◎ GOAL 3

SUB-GOAL:

TINY STEPS

1	☐ 6	☐
2	☐ 7	☐
3	☐ 8	☐
4	☐ 9	☐
5	☐ 10	☐

SUB-GOAL:

TINY STEPS

1	☐ 6	☐
2	☐ 7	☐
3	☐ 8	☐
4	☐ 9	☐
5	☐ 10	☐

SUB-GOAL:

TINY STEPS

1	☐ 6	☐
2	☐ 7	☐
3	☐ 8	☐
4	☐ 9	☐
5	☐ 10	☐

SUB-GOAL:

TINY STEPS

1	☐ 6	☐
2	☐ 7	☐
3	☐ 8	☐
4	☐ 9	☐
5	☐ 10	☐

SUB-GOAL:

TINY STEPS

1	☐ 6	☐
2	☐ 7	☐
3	☐ 8	☐
4	☐ 9	☐
5	☐ 10	☐

SUB-GOAL:

TINY STEPS

1 ☐ 6 ☐
2 ☐ 7 ☐
3 ☐ 8 ☐
4 ☐ 9 ☐
5 ☐ 10 ☐

SUB-GOAL:

TINY STEPS

1 ☐ 6 ☐
2 ☐ 7 ☐
3 ☐ 8 ☐
4 ☐ 9 ☐
5 ☐ 10 ☐

SUB-GOAL:

TINY STEPS

1 ☐ 6 ☐
2 ☐ 7 ☐
3 ☐ 8 ☐
4 ☐ 9 ☐
5 ☐ 10 ☐

SUB-GOAL:

TINY STEPS

1 ☐ 6 ☐
2 ☐ 7 ☐
3 ☐ 8 ☐
4 ☐ 9 ☐
5 ☐ 10 ☐

SUB-GOAL:

TINY STEPS

1 ☐ 6 ☐
2 ☐ 7 ☐
3 ☐ 8 ☐
4 ☐ 9 ☐
5 ☐ 10 ☐

As I mentioned earlier, we are focusing on three goals as a maximum in this plan, but the only person who can know the optimum number of goals you can set yourself is YOU! Someone working full-time with a young family is clearly going to have fewer resources than a person who has just taken early retirement on a healthy pension. Breaking down your end goals into subgoals, then into tiny steps, will give you a reality check so you can see what's feasible. Even if it seems tedious, the planning time for your goals is time well spent and will really make a difference to how easily you succeed.

Take your time to break EVERY step down into the SMALLEST possible component and decide if you need to set rewards for each step / subgoal or each goal. I go on a lot about doing things in ten-minute chunks, but this is because it's a proven strategy that has worked for me and my clients for years. And it's especially good for times when we struggle with motivation! I recently worked with a mum of three who had been widowed, needed to work, run the home and 'be mum **and** dad'. 'Give it Ten' was a complete game-changer for her and enabled her to chip away at all her tasks without that all-engulfing sense of being permanently overwhelmed and stressed. There are times when even five-minute chunks are called for; with a bit of imagination and planning even super busy people can get productive whilst the kettle is boiling, or the microwave is heating a ready meal.

Wrapping things up

Good job! You've got the foundations of your goal process under your belt! Now the time has come to think about WHEN you're going to start, HOW LONG each stage will take and WHEN you aim to have completed your goal.

Roll on **Chapter 4**!!

WHEN IS IT POSSIBLE?

4

What's this chapter about?

This section is all about the importance of the timings of your goal actions. The clearer you get on all the details, the easier they will be to implement.

As with all the P.O.W.E.R. TOOL steps, there is no right or wrong timeframe; the exercises here will help you create one that is realistic for **you**.

Once everything is noted in your action plan diary, all you need to do is complete the pre-planned tasks for each day – no time wasted wondering what you're doing next!

The best time to start?

As we have seen, the more specific we are when setting our goal, the easier it is to achieve it. Being specific also means getting clear on your, 'When?', i.e., when you're starting to work towards your goal, when the different steps are going to happen, and when you will have achieved your goal.

Most of the time the answer to the question, 'When should I start taking action towards my goal?', is NOW!! However, as the P.O.W.E.R. TOOL FOR GOALS® is all about making success as easy as possible, there are some things you will need to consider. Whilst there is no perfect time to start, there are definitely times that will not lead to easily achieved successful outcomes. Everyone is different of course, and some of the following considerations may actually spur certain people on to make changes. This tool is flexible and designed to work for you as an individual, so give some thought to what else is going on in your life and then decide what works best for YOU.

Exercise 1.
Getting ready

Work through the following to get clear on your 'when' and make notes in **Table A**.

Try visualising yourself taking the action steps you created in the previous chapter to get a good idea of whether it feels like the right time to begin.

Think about what else is going on in your life right now and be realistic about what is feasible. Remember the resources we talked about in **Chapter 3**? Go through them and see if you need to do any preliminary work to clear the decks, so to speak:

Time: Is your time already overstretched? Do you need to consider getting up a bit earlier? Are you the sort of person who really can get productive early morning? (Jeff Bezos goes to the office at 10am and that works for him! We're not all able to be up and at 'em from the crack of dawn, so be honest about what works for you.) Can you reduce your working hours? Is there someone who can take care of the kids / walk the dog to free up some time? Do you need to consider nibbling away at your action plan in ten-minute chunks rather than trying to throw longer periods of time at it?

Energy: Are you already feeling burnt out? Are there any existing tasks you need to complete so you can free up mental or physical energy? Can you delegate anything?

Skills / Information: Do you need to do more research? Do you need to do a quick booster course in anything? Are there any action steps that you are able to delegate to someone who is more skilled in certain areas?

Money / Equipment: Have you got the stuff you need for your project? If you need to buy equipment or materials, do you have enough money? Are there debts that need clearing? Do you need to save money first, or side hustle / sell stuff you don't need any more to make a bit extra? Is it appropriate or possible to borrow the money (especially if your goal is an investment such as acquiring a qualification that will increase your income)?

Support: If you are counting on support from others, you will need to know their availability. Are there any organisations that can provide free or paid support of any kind? What about groups on social media? Can you barter or swap services with someone?

Physical Space: Do you already have the space you need? Do you need to repurpose a room, or part of a room? Will you need to declutter to create a space for your project? If you need extra space, is there somewhere you can use for free, or will you need to consider renting space?

This may mean preliminary work in:

- Reviewing your daily or weekly schedule
- Delegating chores where possible
- Subscribing to an app or website that will help you
- Budgeting for your goals
- Sourcing new or used equipment

- Getting a personal trainer
- Hiring a life coach
- Joining a support group
- Clearing out your cupboards of junk food
- Adding relevant actions to your 'Tiny Steps' in Exercise 3 of the previous chapter.

Make your own notes in the table on the next page to see if you're ready to go.

If there is anything that needs addressing you can:

Add it to your list of subgoals

or

do it NOW

or

mark in your diary when you will do it

• • •

If you have gone through the above and think that the time is right but can't seem to get going, you might want to look at the exercises on procrastination and self-sabotage in **Chapter 7**.

TABLE A

TIME

ENERGY

SKILLS/INFORMATION

MONEY/EQUIPMENT

SUPPORT

PHYSICAL SPACE

Exercise 2.
Set your timeframe

There are three options for setting your timeframe:

- Looking at whether there are any external conditions (e.g., loan or lease expiry, retirement, end of sabbatical leave) that create a deadline for your goal
- Choosing a deadline that works for you for other reasons
- If you're not bothered by how long the project will take, simply deciding when you can / want to start

Whichever approach relates to your situation it is CRUCIAL that you commit to a start and / or end time otherwise your goal will just not happen. It is human nature to put off stuff we haven't actually made space for in our mental calendar.

Remember which option you're using and complete the following tables to gain an overview that you will be able to use in your detailed action plan.

Options 1 or 2

If you're working with **Options 1 or 2** you will need to work **backwards** and fit all the steps and subgoals into the time available. This means you will start by putting your goal and end date in the box and work UP the chart by putting your subgoals and dates in the appropriate spaces.

Option 3

If you're going for **Option 3** you will be working **forwards** and will assign subgoals to each time section until you reach your end goal.

> **TIP:** Add all the subgoals from your **Goal Type** table in **Chapter 3** (**not** the Tiny Steps – save those for your action plan in **Chapter 8**) into each week / month / other timeframe in the orange boxes. Note that this time you are writing them down in the order you will actually do them.

Please note that if your goal is longer term (more than a few months) you will just need to adapt your time frames accordingly.

GOAL 1:

_____

WEEK/MONTH 1 / OTHER
ACTUAL DATES / / - / /

_____

WEEK/MONTH 2 / OTHER
ACTUAL DATES / / - / /

_____

WEEK/MONTH 3 / OTHER
ACTUAL DATES / / - / /

_____

WEEK/MONTH 4 / OTHER
ACTUAL DATES / / - / /

_____

GOAL/SUB-GOAL & END DATE:

_____

GOAL 2:

WEEK/MONTH 1 / OTHER
ACTUAL DATES / / - / /

WEEK/MONTH 2 / OTHER
ACTUAL DATES / / - / /

WEEK/MONTH 3 / OTHER
ACTUAL DATES / / - / /

WEEK/MONTH 4 / OTHER
ACTUAL DATES / / - / /

GOAL/SUB-GOAL & END DATE:

GOAL 3:

WEEK/MONTH 1 / OTHER
ACTUAL DATES   /   /   -   /   /

WEEK/MONTH 2 / OTHER
ACTUAL DATES   /   /   -   /   /

WEEK/MONTH 3 / OTHER
ACTUAL DATES   /   /   -   /   /

WEEK/MONTH 4 / OTHER
ACTUAL DATES   /   /   -   /   /

GOAL/SUB-GOAL & END DATE:

Wrapping things up

Another great job done!

Remember that this whole process is flexible, so don't be afraid of committing to time scales – everything can be tweaked or rewritten if it really isn't right, but if you don't write it down the chances are it will never happen.

You really are getting ready to start smashing those goals and the next chapter will give you tips on how to **measure** how you're doing!

EVALUATE AND MEASURE YOUR PROGRESS

5

What's this chapter about?

Here, you'll discover why it's so important to evaluate and measure your progress towards your goals.

The exercises are going to help you find ways that will help you keep an eye on how things are shaping up.

Why bother with feedback?

Evaluating and measuring your progress throughout your action plan gives you the opportunity to check you're on track or confirm that you still feel the goal is important to you. Either way, taking stock will enable you to decide whether to keep going, tweak or change what you're doing – or abandon this goal altogether in favour of another one. It might seem surprising that I mention giving up on a goal, but we have to keep this real and accept that sometimes things don't turn out as we expected. There's absolutely no shame in changing your plans and by using all the steps in this P.O.W.E.R. TOOL FOR GOALS® you will have the confidence to make the right decisions for YOU and not feel obliged to keep going just because you started or feel a failure for dropping something that wasn't working for you.

Just about every scientific study on goal setting has shown the importance of feedback in successful goal outcomes. Whether the feedback comes from a machine (phone app, scales, smart watch, computer programme), from our own assessment or from another person, it encourages us to move on to the next step, the next goal, or will help us revise our action plan. Feedback may 'quantitative' (i.e., can be measured in specific units like losing x pounds / kilograms, being able to run y miles / kilometres, or achieve a particular exam grade) or 'qualitative' (i.e., how you will feel when you reach your goal). They are both equally useful and the important thing is to have built those measures into your plan from the outset. It's also vital to understand that there is no such thing as bad feedback – it is simply a way of knowing whether what you are doing is effective and right for you, or if you need to make any changes.

Some people find they are more motivated if they feel there is some competition to spur them on. This is a very natural and healthy trait provided we don't become obsessed with 'looking over our shoulder' and we don't lose our own connection with the goal. If you have a 'goal buddy', a bit of light-hearted competition can be fun, but I strongly recommend that you don't use comparative measurements as your only way to assess how you're doing – make sure you have some objective measures in place and that you keep track of your own 'personal bests'.

It's one thing to mutually score yourself against someone who knows you are doing it, but it's quite another to secretly compare and measure yourself against friends, family, social media contacts and celebrities. I've lost count of the number of clients who have come to me for help with low self-esteem which has been fuelled by comparisons with people who have publicly shared photos of their 'perfect' life / home / family / holiday. THERE IS NO SUCH THING AS A PERFECT ANYTHING. FACT! I know this from working for years with other clients who post those 'perfect' images because they believe it is expected of them, but inside they may be crippled with anxieties / fears / phobias / depression that they dare not share. So, remember that people show you the highlights, the best bits, the edited bits, and they share images of HOW THEY WISH THEIR LIFE WAS! If you see social media as the 'red carpet of life', you will remember that you are seeing carefully orchestrated pictures of what people want you to see. And that's fair enough! Why shouldn't you glam up for the camera? George Clooney wouldn't rock up to the Oscars in his pj's and Oprah wouldn't wear scruffy sweatpants for a photoshoot, would they?!

To sum up, keeping it real and personal, comparing you one

month or six months ago with you now, truly is the best way to assess how you're doing. I know how damaging our tendency to compare ourselves with fantasies that aren't real is and really want you to remember this as you make changes in your life and reach for your goals. Just be yourself and strive to be a better version of yourself with each day that passes! You are awesome, you are unique, and you are deeply loveable as you are. The changes you are making are FOR YOU. Please don't ever forget this.

Right, now, let's get back to the practicalities of your P.O.W.E.R. TOOL FOR GOALS® evaluation process.

This chapter will encourage you to think about your goals and for each one, decide how you will know:

- When you've achieved your end goal
- If your action steps are working

In order to know the answers, you will obviously need to build measures into your defined goal. There are clearly some changes and goals that are easily measurable, like the quantitative examples above. But it is in fact possible to measure ANY change you want to! If you're not sure how you can make your goal measurable, find some examples of targets you can aim for in different types of goals on the following page.

GOALS – how to measure

To have more 'me time'	I will have one relaxing bath, a 'PJ' night and attend one gym / fitness class each week, plus one meal out with friends per month
Learn to play the guitar	I'll be able to play the basic chords of my chosen song within two months
Declutter home	I will be able to use the dining room to entertain friends in one month
Spend more time with kids / grandkids	I'll have one movie night per week and a day trip one Sunday per month
Reduce social anxiety	I will make small talk for two minutes with a different colleague each day for a week
Change my appearance	I'll book a night out with my partner / friends with a new hairstyle / wearing a new outfit style

Exercise 1.
Plan how you will evaluate your success

Now it's time to think about how you will measure **your** goals.

Look back at your 'Tiny Steps' from **Chapter 3** and your subgoals from **Chapter 4**. See which ones are 'milestones' you can use to measure progress or reword them so you can fill in the following evaluation statements.

Here's an example to show you what I mean:

- **Goal:** to become better at interior design
- **I will know I have achieved this goal because:** I will have completed and passed the ABC online certificate in interior design and will have redesigned my bedroom.
- **Milestones along the way:** Complete each module, revise each module, complete assignments, sit exam, design bedroom, buy furniture.

Goal 1: ....

I will know I have achieved this goal because:

....

....

....

....

Milestones along the way:

....

....

....

Goal 2: ....

I will know I have achieved this goal because:

....

....

....

....

Milestones along the way:

Goal 3:

I will know I have achieved this goal because:

Milestones along the way:

This evaluation stage is not, however, just about 'measuring', it's also an opportunity to check in with your gut feeling and overall impression of how it's going.

> **TIP:** Remember to keep your eye on the bigger picture – studies have shown that this approach leads to success and is a good general indicator of successful outcomes in future goals. Ask yourself each week, 'Why am I working towards this goal?' (See also **Chapter 6**.)

Exercise 2.
Plan how you will review your actions

Note: Have a quick look through this exercise now (so you are aware of what questions you need to think about) but write **your** answers in the tables when you begin actioning your plan in **Chapter 7**.Look at all the goal-related actions you have taken. For each one, ask yourself the following questions and use the **Action Review Charts** to log your answers:

- Did this action feel good or easy?
- Or did it feel uncomfortable in any way?
- Did this action move me towards my goal (even in a small way)?

If the answer is 'Yes', that's fantastic! Think about if you need to repeat more of these actions in the next week.

If the answer is 'No', this is really valuable feedback! Think about why it wasn't useful and what you can learn from the experience. Look ahead to the next week and see if you need to adjust any part of your action plan to reflect this.

Note anything you've learned from your experiences in the last column.

EXAMPLE: ACTION REVIEW CHART

ACTION	HOW DID IT FEEL?	TOWARDS GOAL?	WHAT DID I LEARN?
Daily run	Mostly good but was too much to do every day	Yes	Aim to do 4 or 5 times per week instead of daily
Reading 1 chapter each day	Good but didn't feel enough as some chapters are quite short	Yes	Look ahead and choose which days it's better to read 2 chapters
Yoga before breakfast	Didn't enjoy it – struggled to wake up	No	Look at doing pilates or Tai Chi later in day
Weekly budget check	I felt in control and calm	Definitely!	Keep doing it!
Spending 1-1 time with kids	Kept moving the time due to other commitments	A bit	Need to block it out in everyone's diary and make it non-negotiable!

GOAL 1: ACTION REVIEW CHART

ACTION	HOW DID IT FEEL?	TOWARDS GOAL?	WHAT DID I LEARN?

GOAL 2: ACTION REVIEW CHART

ACTION	HOW DID IT FEEL?	TOWARDS GOAL?	WHAT DID I LEARN?

GOAL 3: ACTION REVIEW CHART

ACTION	HOW DID IT FEEL?	TOWARDS GOAL?	WHAT DID I LEARN?

Wrapping things up

It's all coming together really well, so feel proud of getting this far! Another 'high five' to you!

You're now ready to design your very own **Action Plan** using the guides in **Chapter 7**. You can come back each week to the **Action Review Tables** from **Exercise 2** from this chapter (or download them of course!).

? REASONS WHY YOU'RE DOING THIS?

6

What's this chapter about?

You've got ideas for your goals from **Chapter 1** and now it's time to check in with why you want to achieve them to maximise your chances of success.

Here we'll look at why it's important to know your reasons and commitment and go through a series of questions so you can get clear on your 'why?' and get off to a great start!

The tables are designed to look at up to five of your goals so you can narrow it down to the most important for you. You can of course do more (or fewer) at this point but aim for a minimum of three if you can.

Why do you want to make changes?

If you are clear on your reasons for setting your goals, are sure that fundamentally you are doing it for YOU and follow the P.O.W.E.R. TOOL FOR GOALS® strategy, you can pretty much guarantee a successful outcome.

Even if you want to make changes and achieve goals that will mean a better life for you and your partner / family it has to be because YOU want and believe in this 'improved' lifestyle.

Exercise 1.
Work out what's important to you

Here are a few questions for you to think about as you work through the steps of your P.O.W.E.R. TOOL. There are no right or wrong answers to these questions, but if you are honest in your replies you will be guided by them.

?

Q1 ON A SCALE OF 1-10, HOW IMPORTANT IS THIS GOAL TO YOU?
(1= not important at all, 10 = a real priority for me)

GOAL 1	GOAL 2	GOAL 3	GOAL 4	GOAL 5

Q2 ON A SCALE OF 1-10, HOW COMMITTED ARE YOU
TO MAKE CHANGES AND TAKE ACTION?
(1= not committed at all, 10 = will do anything I can to make this happen)

GOAL 1	GOAL 2	GOAL 3	GOAL 4	GOAL 5

Q3 ON A SCALE OF 1-10, HOW MUCH DO YOU CARE ABOUT
A POSITIVE OUTCOME?
(1= not really bothered, 10 = absolutely want this to happen)

GOAL 1	GOAL 2	GOAL 3	GOAL 4	GOAL 5

Q4 ON A SCALE OF 1-10, WHAT DIFFERENCES WILL THE
ACHIEVEMENT OF THIS GOAL MAKE TO YOUR LIFE?
(1= not much change really, 10 = this goal is life-changing)

GOAL 1	GOAL 2	GOAL 3	GOAL 4	GOAL 5

Q5 ON A SCALE OF 1-10, HOW MUCH DO YOU BELIEVE
YOU WILL ACHIEVE THIS GOAL?
(1= don't really think I can do it, 10 = I am definitely going to smash this)

GOAL 1	GOAL 2	GOAL 3	GOAL 4	GOAL 5

Q6 WRITE DOWN THE NAME OF THE PERSON
WHO HAS CHOSEN THIS GOAL?
(You? / partner? / parent? / teacher? / friend?...)

GOAL 1	GOAL 2	GOAL 3	GOAL 4	GOAL 5

Look back over your answers and sit with them for a few minutes. As I said earlier, there are no right or wrong answers – this is simply one way of working out how likely you are to invest in the goal-setting process.

Now focus on one goal at a time.

If your scores for **Questions 1 – 4** are 6 or less for this goal, you may not be motivated enough to make this happen. Or you may not enjoy the journey. Ask yourself if you can you tweak the definition of the low-scoring goal. Does that increase the score? If so, brilliant! If not, you have two options:

1. Swap the goal for another from your list

2. Assuming you absolutely have to do this, remember that the P.O.W.E.R. TOOL framework will make it as easy as possible for you and you will need to focus on inserting as many rewards as you can into your action plan to sustain your motivation.

If your scores are 7 or above that's fantastic. You're off to a flying start!

Look at your scores for **Question 5**. If you answered 5 or below remember that I will be with you every step of the way throughout this book. If you do all the exercises (including any relevant ones from **Chapter 8**) you will acquire strategies to help you and will see that your goal is broken down into totally manageable chunks.

If your scores are 6 or above, then you already have a great mindset for success and will be able to enjoy that feeling of being in control of your own action plan.

If your name appears in each box for **Question 6** (it's okay if it's alongside someone else's name) that's great news! It is vital that you are personally invested in your goal in order to achieve long-lasting results as I explain below. If your name is not in the box this is a massive red flag and needs to be addressed. Firstly, think again about what **you** will get out of your goal. Even if the outcome appears to only benefit someone else **you** must want it in your heart of hearts.

For example, if you want to make changes and achieve goals that will mean a better life for you and your partner / family it has to be because YOU want and believe in this 'improved' lifestyle. Or maybe your goal is to make some extra money to help your child get to university or on the property ladder. You are choosing to give him / her opportunities (maybe that you didn't have) that will help them have a better life. You will feel proud of giving them a great start to adult life and know that you have done your best for them, and that sense of pride and achievement is what **you** will get out of it.

Internal and external goals

There are many reasons for making changes in your life and setting goals – sometimes we just <u>feel</u> that something needs to be done, like we saw in **Chapter 1**. Sometimes external circumstances give us a nudge (or a great big shove in some cases). We might fail an exam and not have the money to retake it, we may become ill or lose our job. There are also some people who have a 'life plan' from a very early age and need a goal-setting strategy to make this happen. An eighteen-year-old young man attending one of my P.O.W.E.R. TOOL FOR GOALS® workshops described his vision for the next fifteen years with incredible detail and enthusiastically set about applying the tools so he could see how and when each goal would work out.

Goals and life plans may be set internally, externally or collaboratively. When the drive for change and goals comes from within you this is 'internal'. If the plans are set by another person (a parent, teacher, doctor or partner, for example) this would be 'external'. For example, lifestyle changes such as losing weight or stopping smoking may be instigated by a medical professional or a partner. If you embark on a set of life goals with someone else (e.g., saving to buy a home together) this would be collaborative goal setting.

Sometimes there will be a combination of internally, collaborative or externally assigned goals – for example, when told that you must lose weight (primary goal) in order to reduce health risks, you may still be able to decide exactly what changes will be made (your subgoals).

Whatever the 'trigger' for making change, however, it is vital that somewhere inside of yourself there is a true and deep connection to your primary goal to maintain momentum and motivation in your action plan, and in order to sustain your achievement. If that desire is not there, it is unlikely that you will reach your goal or maintain any changes. This was the case of a client who came to me years ago for help with smoking cessation. He had been diagnosed with COPD (Chronic Obstructive Pulmonary Disease), required surgery to save his leg and had been told to stop smoking before they would operate. I was uncertain of his true commitment at the time and would now, as a more experienced therapist, refuse to work with someone with this mindset. However, he desperately wanted the surgery and I was equally eager to help so I agreed to work with him. He did actually stop for a couple of days and then briefly reduced the number of cigarettes he smoked before returning to one-to-two packets a day after the operation. Despite becoming disabled and unwell and being clearly told the risks of continuing to smoke, he did not truly WANT to stop, nor did he or his wife – also a smoker – believe he ever could.

When that true desire for change is present, even when

there are obstacles, it's a different story. Another client came to see me – a lady in her fifties crippled by low self-esteem and depression but with dreams of a better life. She had followed the career path her father had chosen for her and spent decades loathing her job and her life. With therapy and coaching support, she found the confidence and the courage to finally follow her own desires, changed career, and became a completely new person: self-assured, energetic and joyful.

So, understanding how **you** answer the question, 'Why are you doing this?' is vitally important. If it is because someone asked or even told you to do it, or to please someone else, this reason will only get you so far without truly wanting it and believing you deserve it in your heart of hearts. Whether it's changing lifestyle habits, following a passion or going for a promotion, the chances are you won't stick at it unless you really see the point and are invested in the goal. There needs to be that 'lightbulb moment' or 'fire in your belly' to make radical life changes, and this has been backed up by scientific research: studies have demonstrated the positive impact on goal outcomes when there is self-belief, high personal motivation and commitment. This doesn't mean that we need to have high self-esteem to begin with (that often comes once you start achieving your subgoals, or with help from a life coach) but we do need to believe that we **can** make changes and are not simply a victim of external events. Psychologists call this 'self-efficacy' or 'internal locus of control', and Dr Carol Dweck describes it as a 'growth mindset' in her book 'Mindset'. If you really want to make changes, then using this P.O.W.E.R. TOOL FOR GOALS® will give you the strategy and action plan you need to hold on to that belief and stay with the right mindset.

Of course, there are always those curved balls that life has a tendency to throw at us and that can mean that stuff which felt important suddenly doesn't matter, which is why these steps are so important to help us keep checking in with ourselves.

Exercise 2.
More useful questions to ask yourself

Why do I want to make this change / achieve this goal?
  Example answer:

	I want to	**learn to dance**
	so that	**I can dance with my partner at our wedding / anniversary party**

Goal 1: I want to ....

         so that ....

Goal 2: I want to ....

         so that ....

Goal 3: I want to ....

         so that ....

Goal 4: I want to ....

         so that ....

Goal 5: I want to ....

         so that ....

Read this out loud. How do you physically feel when you say the second part of the sentence? For many, this will give you butterflies, a surge of energy or simply make you smile if you're truly connected to your goal.

Remember that some goals will be to benefit other people, e.g. 'I want to move house so that everyone can have their own bedroom', but should still excite YOU and trigger feelings of pride.

Hint: If you can't complete the above sentence and simply state what this goal will bring <u>you</u>, you might want to rethink your goal.

How will I feel once I have achieved my goal?

Example answer: Once I've **learned to dance**, I will feel **proud of myself and will feel a lot fitter**

Goal 1: Once I've achieved my goal, I will feel

....

Goal 2: Once I've achieved my goal, I will feel

....

Goal 3: Once I've achieved my goal, I will feel

....

Goal 4: Once I've achieved my goal, I will feel

....

Goal 5: Once I've achieved my goal, I will feel

This second question is just a 'belts and braces' way of enabling you to check in with the emotions and gut reaction you have to your successful outcome.

It's really important not to worry if your responses to the above questions are not all positive. All feedback is useful. Be guided by whatever comes up for you. Your reaction is the best indicator of whether you need to tweak, completely rethink, or review the timing of your goal.

You also need to be aware of how much social influence can impact our commitment. This can push us to **try** to conform (even if it doesn't feel right for us) or do the opposite and rebel! If you know that your goals are unlikely to be accepted in your social group (family, friends, colleagues) then you can plan for this. If it becomes obvious that this conflict of interests is holding you back, please check through the exercises in **Chapter 8**.

KEEPING TRACK OF YOUR REASONS

	GOAL	REASON	NOTES/ACTION NEEDED
EXAMPLE	Move house	To have more space and a garden	Need to have a proper chat with partner and kids before starting action plan and make sure they are on board

Exercise 3.
Keeping track of your reasons

The table on the opposite page gives you a chance to pull your thoughts together and record a summary of the reasons for your goals. Take a few minutes to think about all your goals and complete the following table (or print off a copy from the usual place: **resources.amandacraven.org/powertoolforlifegoals**).

I've provided an example to get you started.

Wrapping things up

You've worked through some really important and useful questions in this chapter. If you have doubts about any of your goals, just flick back to **Chapter 1**, reread your notes and see what you're really aiming to achieve. You may want to change or reframe some or all of your goals and can then go back through the evaluation questions above.

Once you feel happy with what you've chosen, you're ready to focus on the steps needed to make your goals your reality and can work through **Chapters 2, 3, 4 and 5**.

Congratulations!

You're well on your way to success.

YOUR 28-DAY P.O.W.E.R.

Action Plan

7

What's this chapter about?

This is where the fun really begins! The preparation exercises you have already completed will provide the material you need to develop a personalised, step-by-step action plan for yourself. There is also another copy of the **Action Review Chart** so you can objectively evaluate how things are going for you.

Once completed, all you will have to do is follow your daily plan and watch the magic happen!

• • •

Congratulations!! You are ready to draw up your P.O.W.E.R. TOOL FOR GOALS® action plan and change your life!

All you have to do now is complete the weekly tables with information from the previous chapters and then simply put your plan into action. If you've followed all five stages of the P.O.W.E.R. TOOL, actioning each step will soon feel completely natural and certainly won't feel like a chore or a battle. Eventually, as you become more proficient at setting and smashing goals, you may even find that you won't have to write everything down – just the key points. Whether you are new to goal setting or an old hand, though, you will have to work at it in steps. As Jeff Bezos, Amazon CEO, said on *The David Rubenstein Show*, 'You can't skip steps. You have to put one foot in front of the other. Things take time. There are no shortcuts.'

Remember that this part of your action plan will cover the first twenty-eight days of your goal-setting process. Most goals will take longer than this of course, but this first period is critical and you need to be particularly protective of your resources here. You can download more blank tables for subsequent weeks from the usual place:

resources.amandacraven.org/powertoolforlifegoals

Your resources

Before you complete the charts, it's time to run a final check through your resources (see Chapter 4 if you need a full refresher):

Time: be prepared to block out your diary, even if it's just for ten-minute activities.

Energy: you need to have mental and physical capacity for the tasks you set yourself

Skills / Information: do you know everything you need to know and do you have the right skills for the task?

Equipment / Money: from tools to running shoes, smart phone to a computer that is fit for purpose, you are setting yourself up for failure if you don't have what you need

Support: whether this is a babysitter, dog-walker or a goal buddy who will work towards the same goals, this must be in place before you start

Physical Space: be clear on where you will be actioning your goal-steps

Your 'Plan B'

As you're filling out your action plans spend a few minutes making a contingency plan for each step so you know what to do if there are any unforeseen events. This will also reduce the occurrence of negative 'what if' thought patterns which can undermine our confidence and our efforts.

A contingency plan or Plan B should be quick and simple and can be made using the following model:

If... then...

Examples:

If **I eat some junk food** then **I'll rebalance it with more exercise tomorrow**

If **it's too icy to jog outside** then **I'll do a virtual exercise class indoors**

If **my arthritis pains make it difficult to play the guitar** then **I'll work on some music theory / watch a video lesson instead**

If **I go away on business for a few days** then **I'll take my workout weights with me or use the hotel gym / swimming pool**

If **I overspend on my budget this week** then **I'll reduce my spending next week**

Get the picture?!

> **TIP:** <u>You</u> can choose who to tell about your goals – if anyone! Some research has shown that publicly committing to goals increases your chances of success. It's true that being held accountable can work for some people, but it can also create stress and pressure and makes it difficult to keep your plan flexible if you have 'supporters' tut-tutting from the sidelines. So, if you need to or would like to share, choose your confidantes carefully!

This whole plan is designed to be flexible, and the evaluation step encourages you to review how things are going on an ongoing basis. Make sure that you practise self-compassion throughout the process, cut yourself some slack, and adjust your plan as many times as you need.

Make it as easy as you can to succeed – remove all chocolate or junk food from the cupboards if you're looking to reduce weight, make your workspace as pleasant as possible if you will be using this to achieve your goals, ensure your musical instrument / tools / paints / mountain bike / etc. are easily accessible if these are part of your plan.

Much of achieving goals requires new habits to be acquired. The best way to incorporate new habits into existing routine is to pair the new habit – whether it's going for a walk / jog or practising a new instrument – with something that you already do automatically every day / week. For example, if your goal is to do yoga or meditation every day, you might want to do your short practices just before or just after brushing your teeth.

Keep it small! Tiny steps and small chunks of time. Remember that five or ten minutes of doing something is better than doing nothing. Always.

Instructions for completing the tables

You can complete one week at a time or do all four straight off. If you choose the second option be prepared for a bit of scribbling out / re-typing as you will inevitably find you need to make some adjustments. It's all part of the process so **please don't worry about making changes**.

- Write the actual date of your first week next to Week 1 and recap your goals
- Put your 'Tiny Steps' from **Chapter 3**, **Exercise 3**, into the 'Actions' boxes
- Note down the time (or time of day) plus how long you intend to spend on the action in the next box
- Decide what you are going to pair the action with, or what you will do it before / after to help assimilate new helpful habits
- Add any measures you came up with in **Chapter 5**
- At the end of each day tick every action you have completed
- Look over each completed table and identify any 'weak spots' or potential pitfalls. Make a note of your contingency (If… then…) plan for each one
- Make a note of what you will reward yourself with at the end of each week
- Make any other notes that will help you

Don't forget to use your Action Review Charts each week (see **Chapter 5** or download from: **resources.amandacraven.org/ powertoolforlifegoals**).

EXAMPLE TABLE

GOAL(S): *become an interior designer, learn to play guitar, lose 10 kg*

DAY	ACTIONS	TIME/ HOW LONG	PAIR WITH/ BEFORE/AFTER	HOW I WILL MEASURE	✓
MON	Study & do exercises U1 / Practise guitar / Zumba class	1 hour / 10 mins / 7-8pm	After school-run / Before lunch / While kids at swimming	Complete U1 test / Set timer / Attended class!	☐
TUE	Study & do exercises U2 / Practise guitar / Run 3km	1 hour / 10 mins / 7-8pm	After school-run / Before lunch / After doing kids' tea	Complete U2 test / Set timer / Smartwatch	☐
WED	Guitar lesson / Study & do exercises U3 / Run 3km	30 mins / 1 hour / 7-8pm	After school-run / After lunch / After doing kids' tea	Attend lesson / Complete U3 test / Smartwatch	☐
THU	Study & do exercises U4 / Practise guitar / Spin class	1 hour / 10 mins / 7-8pm	After school-run / Before lunch / While kids at Rainbows	Complete U4 test / Set timer / Attended class!	☐
FRI	Study & do exercises U5 / Practise guitar / Run 4km	1 hour / 10 mins / 6-7pm	After school-run / Before lunch / While kids at Mum's for tea	Complete U5 test / Set timer / Smartwatch	☐
SAT	DAY OFF ENJOY TIME WITH THE KIDS!				☐
SUN	Run 5km / Look over units 1-5 / Practise guitar	45 mins / 1 hour / 10 mins	After breakfast/ kids on bikes / While kids do homework / While dinner in oven	Smartwatch / Do revision test / Play homework piece	☐

Now, over to you!

Remember that it's normal to hesitate about putting your plans in writing. Also remember that this is the best way to be able to look at your actions and goals objectively, so JUST DO IT and see what happens. You are not signing your life away – just getting ready for an exciting new chapter in your life .

WEEK 1

WEEK: /   /

GOAL(S):

DAY	ACTIONS	TIME/ HOW LONG	PAIR WITH/ BEFORE/AFTER	HOW I WILL MEASURE	✓
MON					☐
TUE					☐
WED					☐
THU					☐
FRI					☐
SAT					☐
SUN					☐

WEEK 2

WEEK: /   /

GOAL(S):

DAY	ACTIONS	TIME/ HOW LONG	PAIR WITH/ BEFORE/AFTER	HOW I WILL MEASURE	✓
MON					☐
TUE					☐
WED					☐
THU					☐
FRI					☐
SAT					☐
SUN					☐

WEEK 3

WEEK: / /

GOAL(S):

DAY	ACTIONS	TIME/ HOW LONG	PAIR WITH/ BEFORE/AFTER	HOW I WILL MEASURE	✓
MON					
TUE					
WED					
THU					
FRI					
SAT					
SUN					

WEEK 4

WEEK: /   /

GOAL(S):

DAY	ACTIONS	TIME/ HOW LONG	PAIR WITH/ BEFORE/AFTER	HOW I WILL MEASURE	✓
MON					☐
TUE					☐
WED					☐
THU					☐
FRI					☐
SAT					☐
SUN					☐

Action Review Chart

You can use the following review chart (also in **Chapter 5**) to assess some or all of the action steps you're taking. This is an opportunity to make any changes in your action plan for the following week.

ACTION REVIEW CHART

ACTION	HOW DID IT FEEL?	TOWARDS GOAL?	WHAT DID I LEARN?

Other notes to self

Wrapping things up

Wow! You did it! A big high five to you! Keep this book and your notes close by so you can stay on track as you power through your goals. You'll also be able to look back over your journey and marvel at how far you've come. Don't forget the free resources available on:

resources.amandacraven.org/ powertoolforlifegoals

If you decide you'd like additional coaching support, you will also find information by using the above link.

Either way, I'd love to hear about your journey and the life changes you made! Let me know what goals YOU smashed using the P.O.W.E.R. TOOL FOR GOALS®!

My very best wishes,
Amanda

FEELING STUCK?

What's this chapter about?

To maximise your chances of success, you need to be in the best possible place before starting your P.O.W.E.R. TOOL FOR GOALS® Action Plan.

As we saw in **Chapter 4**, there's no such thing as the perfect place or time, but don't set yourself up for failure by starting on your plan at a time of overwhelming challenges. What you view as obstacles will be different to what others perceive as such, so be kind and fair to yourself when you choose your starting point.

This chapter will help anyone who is stuck in some way but can also be worked through if you just like the 'belts and braces' approach.

• • •

So, what if you've pinpointed the goals you want to go for, followed all the P.O.W.E.R. TOOL steps, created your focused action plan and yet something STILL isn't right?

You may...

- have got off to a flying start but have hit a bump in the road and everything's fallen apart
- keep putting off the start date of your action plan
- be following your action plan but nothing seems to be happening
- doubt your ability to actually see this through

Remember that the whole process is organic and designed to be flexible. If it becomes clear that something isn't working, just change it! There is no such thing as failure when using the P.O.W.E.R. TOOL to set your goals – just opportunities to re-evaluate and tweak as and when needed. Jeff Bezos, CEO of Amazon, has repeatedly – and unashamedly – talked about the hundreds of 'failed' business ideas that Amazon has undertaken. One such project was an Amazon auction site which bombed in no uncertain terms despite several attempts to re-jig. After a year or so Bezos realised that it wasn't meant to be and dropped it to refocus on other services that were moving in the right direction. If this approach is good enough for the richest person on the planet (at the time of writing), then I think it's good enough for the rest of us!

How to get the most out of this chapter

For a quick **refresh**, go through **Exercise 1** first of all and use your notes to review and amend your action plan where needed.

The checklist in **Exercise 2** will enable you to work on your **motivation**, **confidence** and **self-compassion**.

Exercise 3 has some tips if you find yourself **procrastinating** and you can find more **confidence-boosting** ideas in **Exercise 4**.

For some deeper work on **self-sabotage** take a look at **Exercise 5**.

> **TIP:** If you feel unable to work through issues that have come up on your own, you may want to find a professional to help you. As you will have identified the obstacles you're facing you will be able to find someone who has expertise in that particular area.

Exercise 1.
A quick recap of your goals

Start with a quick run through of each part of the P.O.W.E.R. TOOL checklist and make notes you can use to either confirm you're actually on the right track and may just need to be more patient, or to make appropriate changes to your action plan:

P. The first thing to do is to take a few quiet moments to go back to the 'Picture It' stage and see what comes up. Just let any thoughts or feelings surface without trying to filter them or deal with them in any way. Notice what you feel in your body when you think about achieving your goal.

   Notes:

O. Next think about the number of steps / goals you're tackling. Have you left enough time for one new habit or routine to become embedded? Have you been realistic in the time available for each step? Are any of the steps causing conflict and pulling you in different directions instead of working together? Are the steps small enough?

Notes:

....

....

....

....

W. Is your timescale realistic? Maybe something has happened that means you need to change some dates and timings in your action plan? Do you need to re-order the steps?

Notes:

....

....

....

....

E. Have you used clear measures to check your progress? Are you using appropriate ways to evaluate how you're doing? Do you need to change some ways that you are measuring your progress? How are you **feeling** about your goal?

Notes:

R. Check in with your 'why?' questions. Ask yourself the reason for each step you're taking. If it doesn't contribute to the goal in some way you may replace it with another action, or just drop it. Clarify, again, why you want to achieve this goal.

Notes:

Exercise 2.
Be kind to yourself!

This tool is all about finding the right way FOR YOU to make changes in your life. It is not an opportunity to beat yourself up about any perceived weaknesses or failures.

If you're feeling frustrated with what you feel is a lack of progress, you need to first review your plan and make sure you're keeping it realistic (see **Exercise 1**).

Remember that this approach also favours BABY STEPS over big dramatic changes. This can feel tedious at times but it is honestly the best way to make lasting changes and you may need to practise being more patient.

When I became unhappy with my weight and devised my first action plan, I tried to implement three (what I thought were small) changes from the start – increase my daily number of steps, limit drinking alcohol to twice a week and have just one small, sweet treat a day. Reasonable, I thought, and very do-able. Wrong! I felt unhappy and under too much pressure all at once and was very close to saying, 'Sod it!' and just buying the next size up in clothes. But I had those tantalising images in my head about me looking and feeling fabulous in my favourite outfits that had got too tight. So, I decided to focus on my steps the first week, eliminate all but one sweet treat from week 2, and just ensure that I had two consecutive nights off alcohol from week 3. I don't want to give you the impression I have a drink problem or anything – most nights I was just hav-ing one G & T – but there was a lot of other stuff going on in my life at that time and I really enjoyed the wind-down time my

G&T gave me as I transitioned from busy work-mode into evening. Giving myself permission to rework my action plan was a vital part of the goal process.

Ways to be kinder to yourself

By implementing rewards that celebrate each and every small win, and regularly practising kind self-talk, you will steer your focus towards what you **have** achieved and feel proud of yourself for each step forward. Try writing a 'Ta-Dah' list every night when you get in to bed – a bullet-point list of everything you have achieved that day, whether it's small or big things.

Become your own best friend and your biggest champion! Talk to yourself just as you would talk to your own best friend – with compassion, understanding and encouragement. Banish the words 'should' and 'shouldn't' as they are damaging, unhelpful and imply we are being judged! If you catch yourself using harsh words just STOP, soften your tone, and plan how you are going to move forward.

I find it easier to look in a mirror to talk to myself in an encouraging way! Why not give it a go? It might feel a bit strange at first but you will get used to it – remember to hold your head up and smile when you say 'It's going to be okay. You've got this!'

I also give myself 'high-fives' when I complete something that was a struggle, even if my daughters do look at me sideways and say, 'Mum, you're just clapping above your head!' It feels good, though, and makes me smile. See how it feels for you!

Exercise 3.
Get motivated!

If you're struggling to start or are losing motivation, **break down your action steps** into even smaller, more manageable ones. If something feels more do-able we're more likely to do it, and if we've got clear measures in place the feedback we get should spur us on to the next step.

The **'Give it Ten'** strategy is very popular with my clients, and another technique I frequently use myself. The idea is to set your timer for ten minutes and JUST DO (EVEN PART OF) SOMETHING from your action plan – you can also use this technique to get through those days when you're over-whelmed by tasks and chores. It's amazing what you can get done in ten focused minutes and you will have moved yourself forward in some way. Sometimes we get caught up in the momentum and want to do more – if you have the time, go for it! Otherwise, feel proud that you took action even when you weren't feeling it. Some people get through a whole bunch of stuff by taking action for ten minutes, having a reward break (coffee, walk, read, TV) for ten and just alternating throughout the morning / afternoon.

You might also want to look again at the rewards you have incorporated into your action plan and see if you can change them to be more appealing!

Exercise 4.
Boost your confidence

If you find that you are losing faith in your ability to make your desired changes happen, this script that is designed to boost your self-confidence may help you. Repeat this exercise as often as you like.

Read one paragraph at a time then re-close your eyes to carry out that part of the exercise.

🎧 You can find the podcast here if you prefer to listen to this exercise:

resources.amandacraven.org/powertoolforlifegoals

Take a few relaxing breaths – in through your nose and out through your mouth – and close your eyes. Imagine you're in a place where you feel relaxed and happy – maybe somewhere you've been, somewhere you'd like to go, or just an imaginary place that has all your favourite things.

Now invite a role model into your special place. Your role model has already achieved the goals you want to achieve and is ready to help you. They will never criticise or judge you but will gently guide you and celebrate each and every step you take towards your goal.

Some people use their future self as a role model – for others it may be a celebrity or well-known mentor.

Imagine just sitting and talking with your role model or maybe going for a walk with them. Their voice is kindly and understanding, their words inspiring. What are they saying? What are they doing? Remember that they are there just for you. Let yourself absorb their ideas and encouragement.

Now, I'd like you to think back to a time when you felt proud of something you did or when someone complimented you or thanked you for your help. If you can't think of anything in the past think about your future self who has already achieved your goals. Be in that moment right now! Notice how it feels and allow those feelings to become more intense. More magnified. Let this moment grow so big it fills all the space in and around you. When all available space is filled think of a colour you associate with confidence and strength. Just go with the first one that comes to mind!

Let that colour fill all the space around you. Colours have energy. Feel the energy of this colour. Feel it infusing you and firing up your inner confidence. Let that colour become bolder and brighter. From now on every time you see that colour you will feel a surge of energy and confidence. Make sure you have plenty of things of that colour around you – clothing, accessories, home furnishings, desk accessories, crystals, plants or flowers – whatever you can think of!

Exercise 5. (🎧)
Working through self-sabotage

Some of my clients who become aware that THEY are often the only ones who are sabotaging their efforts describe it as 'tripping themselves up'. There are so many reasons why we can stand in our own way and most of the reasons are based on fears of some sort. Fear of failure is very common, but did you know that fear of success is just as common and sometimes even harder to deal with? If we are successful in reaching our goals and making changes in our lives, there is a chance that we will leave others behind or be seen as an outsider. The fear of being isolated in our success is very real for many and we can feel that there are different parts of us that want different things – some parts then appear to sabotage the efforts of the parts that do want change, we can't move forward and may be tempted to give up on our goals.

In order to really understand what self-sabotage is, we first need to understand that we are made up of many different 'parts' which ideally work in harmony to create balance and strength and move us towards our life goals. For example, we may have a 'part' that wants to lose weight and another that is rebelling against a partner or parent who is critical of our size. In other cases, we might want to study more but worry about being the only one in our friendship group who goes to college and become afraid of leaving our friends behind.

In order to better understand why **you** are tripping yourself up you could ask yourself:

- Who are you being disloyal to if you achieve your goal?

- Who might you leave behind if you are successful?

- Do you remember being told as a child that you're 'not very clever / funny / confident' or overhearing others talking about you in this way?

- How easy is it for you to complete the following sentence? 'I don't deserve to be successful because

....

....,'

A middle-aged client of mine who wanted to get motivated to move out of her parents' home had been in therapy for years before coming to see me. She had been bullied as a young child and still felt, aged almost fifty, that people were mocking her and that she'd never make anything of herself. When we identified the key parts that were keeping her 'frozen', she was able to see the conflict between the rough and tumble girl she'd been before the bullying began and the shy, introverted woman who had no self-confidence that she'd become. By living like a hermit, she was protecting herself from being judged by others but also suppressing the energy and sense of adventure that was still inside. All the parts within us have good intentions and simply want to protect us from any form of threat (perceived or real). Once we are able to see this, we can accept all our parts – even the ones that appear to hold us back – and use visualisation techniques to encourage them to work together in a more balanced way. In the case of my client, she allowed her more boisterous, playful side to grow and 'have a voice', and the shy, retiring side naturally reduced until she felt a sense of balance and excitement about putting her plans into action.

You can access and listen to my podcast (**resources.amandacraven.org/powertoolforgoals**) for free if you feel there is a part of you that is sabotaging your efforts, and see if that is enough to help you. If you have experienced trauma of some kind and have not yet worked through this, I strongly advise you to seek professional help. To use a more in-depth form of Parts Therapy that is introduced in the podcast I recommend you find a certified Clinical Hypnotherapist who practises this.

When you've listened to the podcast complete the following sentence:

- Everyone deserves to enjoy life and reach their goals. So why not me? I deserve to be successful at

because

Exercise 6.
Re-affirming your goals

Sometimes we get stuck because we lose connection with the desired end result. This exercise will help you reconnect with your goal.

Close your eyes. Use the previously practised visualisation techniques to see yourself having achieved your goal(s) or listen to the podcast 'Visualise your Goal' from **Chapter 2**. Imagine that you are basking in that moment, feeling proud and so good about yourself. Take as long as you need.

Open your eyes and fill in the blanks:

I am so proud of myself for having achieved my goal(s) of

....

....

....

....

....

....

I am thankful that I am now able to

My life is

I feel

Wrapping things up

Find a quiet space to think over everything that has come up for you whilst working through this chapter. If you feel fired up and energised, please go (back) to your **Action Plan** and check what needs tweaking. If you need a breather, take as long as you need.

If you've realised that you do need some extra support, then you need to get that in place and come back to this book – and your **Action Plan** – once you're ready.

Bibliography

Asma, Stephen. 2017. *The Evolution of Imagination*. The University of Chicago Press, Chicago and London

Burton, Lisa and Lent, 2016. Jonathan. 'The Use of Vision Boards as a Therapeutic Intervention', *Journal of Creativity in Mental Health*, 11:1, 52-65, DOI: 1.

Chad J. Donahue, M. F. 2018. 'Quantitative assessment of prefrontal cortex in humans relative to nonhuman primates', *Proceedings of the National Academy of Sciences*, 115.

Hyatt, M. 2018. *Your Best Year Ever*. Grand Rapids: Baker Books.

Kolb, B. 2010. 'Do All Mammals Have a Prefrontal Cortex?', *Evolution of Nervous Systems*, 3, 443-450.

Latham, G. P., & Locke, E. A. 2006. 'Enhancing the Benefits and Overcoming the Pitfalls of Goal Setting', *Organizational Dynamics*, 35(4), 332-340.

Latham, G. P., & Locke, E. A. 2013. Goal Setting Theory, 1990. In G. P. Edwin A Locke, *New Developments in Goal Setting and Task Performance*. Abingdon: Routledge.

Munroe-Chandler, K., & Guerrero, M. 2017. 'Psychological Imagery in Sport and Performance'. *Oxford Research Encyclopaedia of Psychology*. (Retrieved 14 Jul. 2021, from oxfordre.com/psychology/view/10.1093/acrefore/9780190236557.001.0001/acrefore-9780190236557-e-228)

Renner, F., Ji, J. L., Pictet, A., Holmes, E. A., & Blackwell, S. E. 2017. 'Effects of Engaging in Repeated Mental Imagery of Future Positive Events on Behavioural Activation in Individuals with Major Depressive Disorder'. *Cognitive therapy and research*, 41(3), 369–380. (doi.org/10.1007/s10608-016-9776-y)

Renner, F., Murphy, F. C., Ji, J. L., Manly, T., & Holmes, E. A. 2019. 'Mental imagery as a "motivational amplifier" to promote activities'. *Behaviour research and therapy*, 114, 51–59. (doi.org/10.1016/j.brat.2019.02.002)

Vance, A. (n.d.). Elon Musk: *How the Billionaire CEO of SpaceX and Tesla is Shaping our Future*. London: Virgin Digital (Ebury Publishing).

White, T. 2018. *Stanford Medicine* (med.stanford.edu/news/all-news/2018/02/talking-to-doctors-about-your-bucket-list-could-advance-care-planning.html)

Winfrey, O. 2019. *The Path made Clear: Discovering your life's Direction and Purpose*. Bluebird.

About the Author

A highly-qualified hypnotherapist and life coach, Amanda Craven is well-versed in helping individuals get ready for change, overcome obstacles and exceed their goals. After a breast cancer diagnosis at 41, followed by a difficult divorce, Amanda 're-created' herself. Combining her life experiences and her professional training she truly believes in the message she's sharing and wants to be part of her readers' and clients' journey of change, no matter how big or small the change might be.